Piano Concertos Nos. 4 and 5 ("Emperor")

With Orchestral Reduction for Second Piano

LUDWIG VAN BEETHOVEN

EDITED BY FRANZ KULLAK

DOVER PUBLICATIONS, INC.
NEW YORK

Dr. Theodore Baker (1851–1934), translator of Franz Kullak's notes from the German editions of 1883 and 1889, was literary editor and translator for G. Schirmer, Inc., New York, from 1892 to 1926. He is best known for his *Baker's Biographical Dictionary of Musicians* (1900), a standard reference work still in print.

Bibliographical Note

This Dover edition, first published in 1995, is a new compilation of two scores originally published separately by G. Schirmer, Inc., New York, 1901. Piano Concerto No. 4, including three cadenzas by the composer, was originally published as Vol. 624 of Schirmer's Library of Musical Classics under the title *Ludwig van Beethoven/Op. 58/Concerto No. IV/For the Piano/Provided with Fingering, and with a Complete Arrangement, for Piano, of the Orchestral Accompaniment by Franz Kullak/ The Introduction and Notes translated from the German by Dr. Theodore Baker.*

Piano Concerto No. 5, with the same credits for editing and translation, was originally published as Vol. 625 of the same series under the title *Op. 73/Concerto No. V/For the Piano.* There is no reference to the subtitle "Emperor" in either the titling or notes to this edition. The English translations by Baker were based on the German texts in the "new revised" editions of 1883 (Concerto No. 4) and 1889 (Concerto No. 5).

The Dover edition adds: a unified table of contents; lists of instruments, with references to the names and abbreviations used in the orchestral reductions; a more clearly separated section for the cadenzas; and movement numbers throughout. Information about each concerto and the cadenzas, originally confined to first score pages, has been redistributed for easier reference. A new editorial note identifies names and terms used in the footnotes. Page numbers in the footnotes have been changed (and corrected where necessary) to conform to the Dover pagination.

Library of Congress Cataloging-in-Publication Data

Beethoven, Ludwig van, 1770–1827.
  [Concertos, piano, orchestra, no. 4, op. 58, G major; arr.]
  Piano concertos nos. 4 and 5 ("Emperor") / Ludwig van Beethoven ; edited by Franz Kullak ; with orchestral reduction for 2nd piano.
    Score   cm.
  Originally published separately: New York : G. Schirmer, 1901.
  Includes cadenzas for Concerto no. 4 by the composer.
  ISBN 0-486-28442-5
  1. Concertos (Piano)—2-piano scores. I. Kullak, Franz, 1844– 1913. II. Beethoven, Ludwig van, 1770–1827. Concertos, piano, orchestra, no. 5, op. 73, E♭ major; arr. III. Title.
  M1006.B4 op. 58 1995   94-34214
                                                                  CIP
                                                                    M

Manufactured in the United States of America
Dover Publications, Inc., 31 East 2nd Street, Mineola, N.Y. 11501

```
Joseph Patelson Music House                    Invoice No.    35535
160 West 56th Street                              Date: 02/11/08
New York, NY 10019                              Page No.         1




Sold  WENDY H MUSK
 To   23 EQUESTRIAN RIDGE
      NEWTOWN, CT 06470




Cust 17720        Ship date ASAP
Salesman TEM
----------------------------------------------------------------------
Quantity Unit   Item Number        Description        Price  Unit  Extension
----------------------------------------------------------------------
      1 EACH P                BEETHOVEN PIANO CONCERTO  11.95 EACH  (Ordered)
                             NO.4 MINI SCORE EULENBERG
      1 EACH P                BEETHOVEN PIANO CONCERTO  14.95 EACH  (Ordered)
                             4 &5 2PNOS DOVER
      1 EACH S-HAND           HANDLING                   5.00 EACH  (Ordered)
      1 EACH S-SHP            SHIPPING UPS 3LBS          5.59 EACH  (Ordered)
```

```
----------------------------------------------------------------------
                                                  Sale Amt      37.49
Str:      Reg:      Drw:200   Usr:FL    11:21
                                                  Sales Tax       .00

Cred    37.49 ***********4007   0311   Auth:106503    Total      37.49
                                                  Pmt Rec'd     37.49
                                                  Bal Due         .00
              **ORDER COMPLETE**
```

CONTENTS

NOTE

Editor FRANZ KULLAK (1844–1913) succeeded his father, the celebrated teacher Theodor Kullak, as director of the Neue Akademie der Tonkunst, Berlin, specializing in the training of pianists. In his notes to this edition, he refers to the following people and terms, which are here explained:

"APPENDIX": Three Original Cadenzas for Piano Concerto No. 4, p. 71.

"AUTOGRAPH": For Concerto No. 5, the original full score, in the Berlin Royal (now State) Library.

CARL CZERNY (1791–1857): Beethoven's student and Franz Liszt's teacher, wrote *Complete Theoretical and Practical Pianoforte School*, Op. 500 (1839), a summary of pianistic styles and techniques of his time. (Kullak refers to it as "Pianoforte-Method.") "Die Kunst des Vortrags" ["The Art of Execution"] is its supplement. Czerny's comments about the Piano Concerto No. 4 are quoted by Thayer (see below).

JOSEPH FISCHHOF (1804–1857) gathered one of the great private collections of eighteenth and nineteenth-century music manuscripts, including Bach's cantatas and Beethoven's works. After his death, his library was sold to the Berlin Royal (now State) Library. See footnotes, pp. 73, 79, 80.

GUSTAV NOTTEBAUM (1817–1882) prepared the *Thematic Catalogue of Beethoven's Works*, published by Breitkopf & Härtel, 1865.

"ORIGINAL EDITIONS": For Concerto No. 4, the full score published by Kunst-und Industrie-Comptoir, Vienna and Perth, 1808. For Concerto No. 5, three different impressions of the full score published by Breitkopf & Härtel, 1811. Kullak's notes also refer to early editions by C. F. Peters ("P.") and by T[obias] Haslinger, and to a Breitkopf & Härtel ("Br. & H." or "B. & H.") edition of Concerto No. 5 by Ignaz Moscheles (1794–1870), a renowned pianist-composer and teacher.

ALEXANDER WHEELOCK THAYER (1817–1897): Author of *The Life of Ludwig van Beethoven* (3 volumes, including a Chronological Catalogue): German edition, 1866; English editions, 1921 and 1964.

"TUTTI" and "TUTTI-ARRANGEMENTS": A reduction of the orchestra score, printed in small notes in the solo part (Piano I). See Kullak's comments, p. 83: The autograph of Piano Concerto No. 5—in which the *tutti* are indicated ". . . by figured basses [*continuo*] . . . together with melody-notes and occasional harmony-notes . . ."—carries on the eighteenth-century function of the keyboard player as both principal performer and *ripieno*, the "reinforcing section" of the ensemble, doubling the orchestral bass line and other voices between solo passages. Kullak's elaborations, based on a Breitkopf & Härtel full score, best serve the modern soloist as a continuous orchestral cue. Today's performances with large orchestras render the *ripieno* function of the solo part unnecessary.

Piano Concerto No. 4 in G Major

OP. 58 (1805–6)

FOURTH CONCERTO.

Dedicated to his Imperial Highness Archduke Rudolph of Austria.★

Finished 1806(?). Published in August, 1808, by the Kunst-und Industrie-Comptoir, Vienna and Pesth. Performed for the first time in public by the composer on Dec. 22, 1808, in the Theater an der Wien. According to Thayer (Life of Beethoven, vol. III. pp. 6-8), this concerto was played as early as March, 1807 in the salons of Prince L(obkowitz).

★In the original edition in oblong form, the complete title, surrounded by a wreath, reads: *"Viertes /Concert/ für das Pianoforte/ mit 2 Violinen, Viola, Flöte, 2 Hautbois, 2 Clarinetten, / 2 Hörnern, 2 Fagotten, Trompetten* [sic], *Pauken, /Violoncell und Bass. /Seiner Kaiserlichen Hoheit, dem/Erzherzog Rudolph von Oesterreich/ unterthänigst gewidmet von L./van Beethoven./Op. 58.* [Outside the wreath, to the left]: *592.* [Below]: *Wien und Pesth im Verlage des Kunst und Industrie Comptoirs."* [No price given.]

Instrumentation

[The orchestral reduction contains instrument names and abbreviations listed below.]

Woodwinds [Wind]
    Flute [Fl.]
    2 Oboes [Ob.]
    2 Clarinets [Cl.]
    2 Bassoons [Bssn., Bn., B. (*also used for Bass*)]

Brass
    2 Horns [Hn.]
    2 Trumpets [Tr.]

Percussion
    Timpani [Tp.]

Solo Piano

Strings [Quartet, Q. = Violins I, II, Violas, Cellos]
    Violins I, II [Vl.]
    Violas [Viola]
    Cellos [Violoncello, Vlc.]
    Basses [B. (*also used for Bassoon*)]

I.

(1) Carl Czerny, "Die Kunst des Vortrags", Supplement to the great Pianoforte-Method op. 500.
(2) 1 Flute, 2 Oboes, 2 Clarinets, 2 Horns, 2 Bassoons, and Strings (Q.)   Trumpets and Drums not till last movement.

(1) All appoggiaturas in this Concerto, with the sole exception of that beginning the trill $\widehat{tr}$ on p. 69, are *crossed* in the original edition; whereas the original impression of the C-minor Concerto, which was published by the same firm 4 years previously, contains only uncrossed appoggiaturas.

(2) The f added to this chord in recent editions (likewise a preceding *cresc.*) is not given in the original impression.

(3) To facilitate the study (or memorizing) of the shorter Tutti for the soloist, they are given in his part in a simplified form.

(2) It is evident that the trill-signs (in parenthesis) and the light slurs were merely forgotten in the original edition.
(3) Compare Note on p. 22 .

(1) Often, in later editions, *fp*.
(2) Here also frequently *fp*.

(1) In some editions this f reads $f\!f$, in correspondence with the parallel passage found on p. 32, which, however, is more heavily orchestrated.

(2) p, in correspondence with the parallel passage in some editions, is omitted in the original edition. Also see Note on p. 32.

(1) The reading in the original edition, ![engraver's error notation], which is reproduced in some later ones, we consider to be an engraver's error.

(1) Breitkopf & Härtel, and Peters, repeat the "℘℘." 6 times every other measure. — Czerny says, furthermore (Thayer, II, 348): "He [Beethoven] employed the pedal very often, much more than is indicated in his works".

(1) Properly ◁━━━. Most accents of this kind were given in this form, particularly in the last movement; while, on the other hand, an accent-sign probably meaning a simple diminuendo occurred on p. 8:

(1) In the Orig. Edition these measures read as follows:

On this head we remark:

(a) Differing from our present usage, both the expression-marks and all notes for the left hand, in the Tutti, are as large as those in the Soli.

(b) In the arrangement of the Tutti, the bass part is but very seldom doubled in the lower octave (double-bass part).

(c) The *ff* in the third measure is not given at all in the score at this point, but does occur instead of the *f* in the first of these three measures.

(d) Although the entrance of the solo part is sufficiently indicated (at least for the right hand) by the word "Solo", Czerny nevertheless writes (in his "Kunst des Vortrags") the whole of this third measure in large notes:

"The theme {   } in the first two measures with the greatest possible energy".

(It looks as if Czerny had written from memory; in the notation, at least, he does not follow the printed text [𝄢 instead of 𝄢].)
We shall not decide, whether Beethoven played this last measure, at the public performance with orchestra, in the complete form indicated by Czerny. Also compare a similar passage in the last movement, p. 62.

(1) Br. & H., also Peters, give "*p* 𝄆"; omitted in the original.

(1) Given wrongly ℘ in the original edition.

(1) Br. & H., also Peters, give "dolce", in correspondence with the parallel passage on p.10 .
(2) This "cresc." follows the above, and T. Haslinger.

(1) Variant after Breitkopf & Härtel, like the parallel passage on p.11, employing d^4:

(1) This *p* follows recent editions, like the parallel passage on p. 11; then *pp*.

(1) Br. & H. give [music notation] (not in the score), like the parallel passage [music notation] on p.12.

(1) Though reluctant to deviate from Beethoven's original readings, we find this variant of recent editions the more deserving of consideration from the fact, that by the omission of the note d^1, then not at the composer's command, the point of the original thought (*cf.* the parallel passage on p.13) is, so to speak, broken off. On the other hand, this fact appears to throw special light on the repeated *p* (not found in the parallel passage); for here, according to the original reading, the highest tone g^3, in *forte*, would be apt to drown the melody-tone *d* of the flute, whereas in the parallel passage the *a* of the oboe, besides its greater natural intensity, is essentially reinforced by the closing chord of the pianoforte.——
We advance no opinion as to whether the repeated *p* might have been merely forgotten, in the parallel passage.

(1) Acc. to the parallel passage, ⸙ or ⸙

(1) In Br. & H., and P., likewise with ⌢.
(2) 2 Cadenzas by Beethoven; see Appendix [71].

(1) Compare Czerny's remark touching Beethoven's use of the pedal in the Largo of the C-minor Concerto (p. 23 of our edition). Without abating our reverence for the immortal master, we cannot avoid recognition of the rules for the modern employment of the pedal, requiring a more frequent change or interruption of its effect.

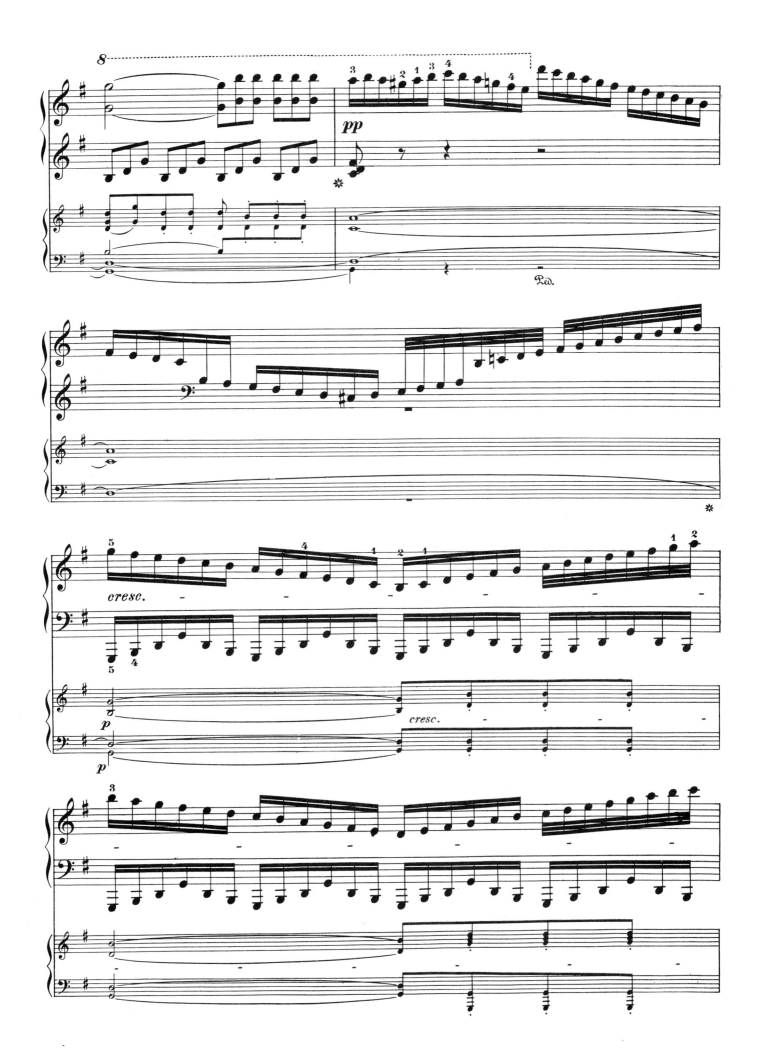

II.

Andante con moto. ♪=100. (Czerny: ♪=84.)

Dans tout cet Andante on tient levée la Pédale, qui ne fait sonner qu'une corde.
Au signe ℟. on lève outre cela les étouffoirs. (1)

(1) "Throughout this *Andante* keep the pedal lifted which allows only one string to sound. At the sign ℟., likewise lift the dampers." [This means: Hold down the soft pedal throughout this *Andante;* take the loud pedal at the sign ℟.]

(2) Czerny sets a "*pp*" before this "*molto cantabile*"; these two directions appear hardly congruous, especially as the soft pedal was already required.

(3) Recent editions, which indicate the Tutti only as interpolations in the Solo part, give "*pp*" here and in the **6** following solo entrances. The original edition, which carries on the orchestral accompaniment uninterruptedly from this point to the close on two staves above the solo part, fills out the hiatuses in the latter with rests, and provides no new expression-mark for the successive later solo entrances.

(1) ? ; Br. & H., and Peters, correct thus:

(2) An effect practicable only on a trichord pianoforte with *shifting*-pedal. [2, and then 3 strings]

2 et puis [2, and then 1 string]
1 corde
dim. sino
al pianiss.

Tutti

Solo   Tutti   Solo

Segue il Rondo.

(1) It is probably a mere mistake that the original edition gives a bar here (end of the page). Br. & H. give a. 𝄐 over the last *tr*; Peters ditto.

(2) In the original edition, probably mistake:

III.

Rondo.

Vivace. ♩ = 132. (Czerny: ♩ = 138.)

(1) Czerny adds *mf.*

(1) Br. & H., likewise Peters (the latter, however, not in the score), correct, in correspondence with the parallel passage on p. 57, $\begin{smallmatrix}8\end{smallmatrix}$ etc. Here the original edition gives only f♯.

(1) Br. & H.'s score adds an *f* at the first eighth-note in the bass.
(2) We add this *f*, following Br. & H. and Peters, in correspondence with the parallel passage on p. 57, also taking into consideration the *f* in the Violoncello and Violin I.

(1) In the parallel passage, p. 58, only *f*.

(1) ⌐ and the figures were added by the editor to facilitate reading.
(2) In B. & H., and Peters, the direction *"ad libitum"* is added to this Cadenza.

(1) *cresc.*, acc. to the analogous passage on p.49 . B. & H. also give ◁

(1) Acc. to the Orig. Edition: etc. See Note on p. 24.

(2) Here, too, the original edition gives *ad lib.*

(1) "Let the Cadenza be short."— For Cadenza by Beethoven, see Appendix [71].

(1) Fingering by Czerny.

(1) "and in the closing measures, *accelerando*"(?). — For the rest, this direction would be in keeping with an observation by Ferdinand Ries concerning the piano-playing of his teacher, Beethoven: "....In general he himself played his compositions very capriciously, but usually kept strict time, only occasionally (though seldom) somewhat pressing the tempo" (Thayer, II, 346.)

Touching the "capriciousness" of his playing, Czerny says: "Astonishing as was his extempore playing, he was often less happy in the performance of his engraved compositions; for, never having time or patience to restudy anything, his success depended chiefly on chance and caprice." (Thayer, II, 348.)

(1) The unrhythmical (as well as indistinct) slurring of the original edition (1, 2, 2, 3 or 3, 2, 3 measures) seemed to us unnecessary of imitation. Both Br. & H. and Peters also slur groups of four measures.

THREE ORIGINAL CADENZAS
FOR PIANO CONCERTO NO. 4

(1809?)

In Nottebohm's Thematic Catalogue of Beethoven's compositions, these Cadenzas are enumerated among the authentic ones; the autographs, according to the same authority, are in the possession of Breitkopf & Härtel. Not published during the composer's lifetime, they were first printed, to the best of our knowledge, by the above firm.

First Cadenza for Movement I
(p. 35)
"Cadenza (ma senza cadere)" [1]

(1) Acc. to Nottebohm, this title was written by Beethoven himself. Also *cf.* Thayer's Chronological Catalogue, Nº 131.

(2) Br. & H. give *f* instead of *d,* probably by mistake (once). The Fischhof copy, in the Berlin Royal Library, reads like our edition.

Second Cadenza for Movement I
(p. 35)

(1) Acc. to Czerny (Pianoforte‑Method, Part I), the auxiliary note of the trill coincident with the melody‑note may be omitted.

Tempo I.

dolce

sf

(1) Another copy, in a different hand from the one in Prof. Fischhof's literary remains (R. Library, Berlin), repeats the last three notes once more.

Cadenza for the Rondo
(p. 66)

(1) "Ped.", according to a copy (by the same hand as the foregoing) in Prof. Fischhof's literary remains. Moreover, in this copy, the $\frac{2}{4}$ time does not begin until the entrance of the following passage in 16th- notes. Besides the above cadenzas, the Fischhof MSS. also include three smaller ones, one to the first movement of this Concerto, and two to the last.

Piano Concerto No. 5 in E-flat Major
("emperor")
op. 73 (1809)

Notes to Beethoven's Concerto in E flat

By FRANZ KULLAK

The present edition of this Fifth Concerto is the result of renewed revision. Besides comparison with the Autograph of the score (in the Royal Library, Berlin), we have collated the text with three different impressions of the original edition published by Breitkopf & Härtel, register [running number of publication] 1613, which we shall call A, B and C respectively. All three impressions were taken from the same plates; though C was provided with a new title-page. Impressions A and B* are quite similar externally; but in B a considerable number of errors are corrected, these errors being, in fact, of such a kind (to judge by the autograph of the score, at least) that they ought properly to have been corrected before the publication of A. As for the other corrections contained in B, there can hardly be a doubt, judging from external and internal evidence†, that they are directly traceable to the composer's own intentions. These changes, of course, are likewise to be found in C. Moreover, we give in the present edition as complete a list as possible of the differences between the Autograph and the Original Editions, and also between these latter, omitting, of course, mere mistakes in writing and engraving. Here we shall take note of one special case, for which there was no room in the foot-notes. The following passage [on p. 95, etc.] has (at least with regard to the non-staccato notes)

the following notation in all the original editions :

In the Autograph, the slurs in the third measure (at N. B.) are altered and prolonged by very heavy strokes, followed in our text and other recent editions. In fact, the original slurring appears to have been [Autogr. (former notation)]:

the staccato may have been added later. Touching the staccato we should also observe, that the original editions do not admit of a consistent discrimination between the signs • • • • and ' ' ' ' The former appear only in isolated instances. A few dots in the Adagio proved to be dashes in the Autograph.

Finally, with regard to the Tutti, it will be of interest to learn that they are indicated, in the piano-part of the Autograph, and similarly in the Original Editions, by figured basses with large note-heads, together with melody-notes and occasional harmony-notes in smaller notes. The Tutti-arrangements in the present edition were made by the editor after a Breitkopf & Härtel score in large 8vo.

Berlin, 1882. F. K.

---

* Their title, mostly in italics, reads literally : " *Grand / Concerto / Pour le Pianoforte / avec Accompagnement / de l'Orchestre / composé et dedié / à Son Altesse Imperiale / Roudolphe / Archi-Duc d'Autriche etc. / par / L. V. Beethoven / Propriété des Éditeurs / Oeuv.* [sic !] *73.*————*Pr. 4 Rthlr. / à Leipsic / Chez Breitkopf & Härtel.*"—Compare herewith Nottebohm's Thematic Catalogue of Beethoven's compositions (2nd Ed.), in which the title of the edition of May, 1811, is given word for word like the above (though omitting statement of price, and slightly deviating in orthography and punctuation). As to time of publication, also *cf.* the "Intelligenzblatt zur Allg. Mus. Zeitung" of 1811. In No. II (February) — the Concerto is advertised to appear

"shortly." In No. VI (May 22), it is announced as published; whereas in No. V (May 8), no mention is made of it.—The title of impression C (printed in the forties) begins with the words: "Cinquième Concerto."—A still later edition by Moscheles, distinguished as a "nouvelle édition" (Breitkopf & Härtel), has the register 7738, and appeared toward the end of the forties.

† *Cf.* a fragment of a letter written by Beethoven and printed in Nohl's "Neue Briefe Beethovens" (Stuttgart, 1867) as No. 60; also the composer's letter of May 6 to the publishers, printed by Thayer (Life of Beethoven, iii, 166).

FIFTH CONCERTO.

Dedicated to His Imperial Highness Archduke Rudolph.

Composed 1809. Published 1811, by Breitkopf & Härtel.

Instrumentation

[The orchestral reduction contains instrument names and abbreviations listed below.]

Woodwinds [Wind]
    Flute [Fl.]
    2 Oboes [Ob.]
    2 Clarinets [Cl.]
    2 Bassoons [Bssn., Bn., B. (*also used for Bass*)]

Brass
    2 Horns [Hn.]
    2 Trumpets [Tr.]

Percussion
    Timpani [Tp.]

Solo Piano

Strings [Quartet, Q. = Violins I, II, Violas, Cellos]
    Violins I, II [Vl.]
    Violas [Viola]
    Cellos [Violoncello, Vlc.]
    Basses [B. (*also used for Bassoon*)]

I.

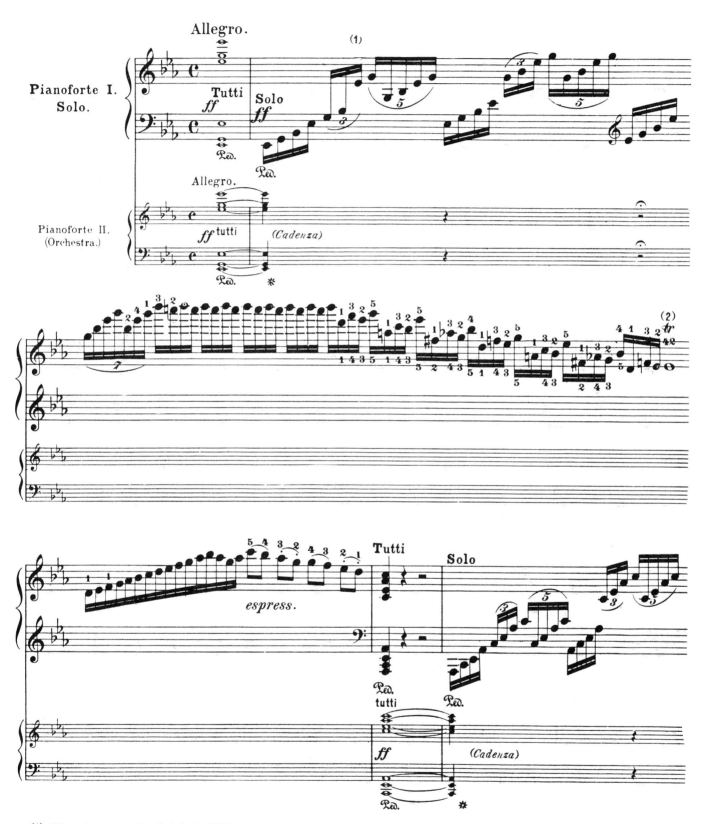

(1) Fingering from the Original Editions.
(2) On the execution of the trill, see Introduction to Op. 15.

(1) The *light* slurs (also given thus in the Autogr.) in the bass staff are omitted in the orig. editions.

(2) In the last two measures the notation for the right hand, in the orig. editions, runs (improperly) thus:

(1) This *f* is repeated in the Autogr.

(1) Acc. to the Autogr., "*sforzato*," in the orig. editions only *sfz* is given here, but further on *sforzato*.

(1) On the employment of the pedal *cf.* the Notes to Op. 37 p. 23, and Op. 58, pp. 15 and 34 of our edition.

(2) ⌐ Fingerings of the orig. editions.

(1) *f* in analogy with the parallel passage on p.112 (omitted in all sources).

(1) Here an "*sf*" is given (probably by mistake) in the original editions.
(2) Repeated in the orig. editions.

(1) This ✻ follows the parallel passage and the Autogr. (omitted in the orig. editions).

(1) **Execution, on our modern pianos:**

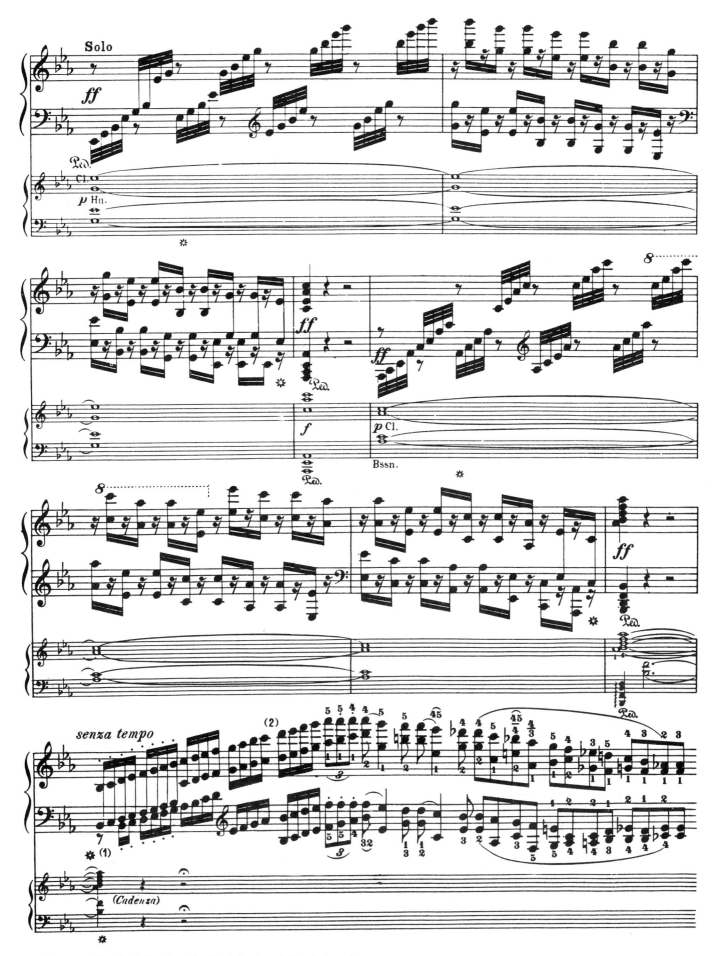

(1) In Edition B, ✱ is given (omitted in A and the Autogr.).
(2) A bar given here in the orig. editions is omitted in the Autogr. (erased: end of the page).

(1) In large note-heads, in the orig. editions.

(1) In the Autogr., and likewise in the paralled passage in the orig. editions, ✻

(1) *8va bassa* on our modern pianos.

(2) Edition A gives [musical notation] (ditto in the Autogr.); Edition B: [musical notation]

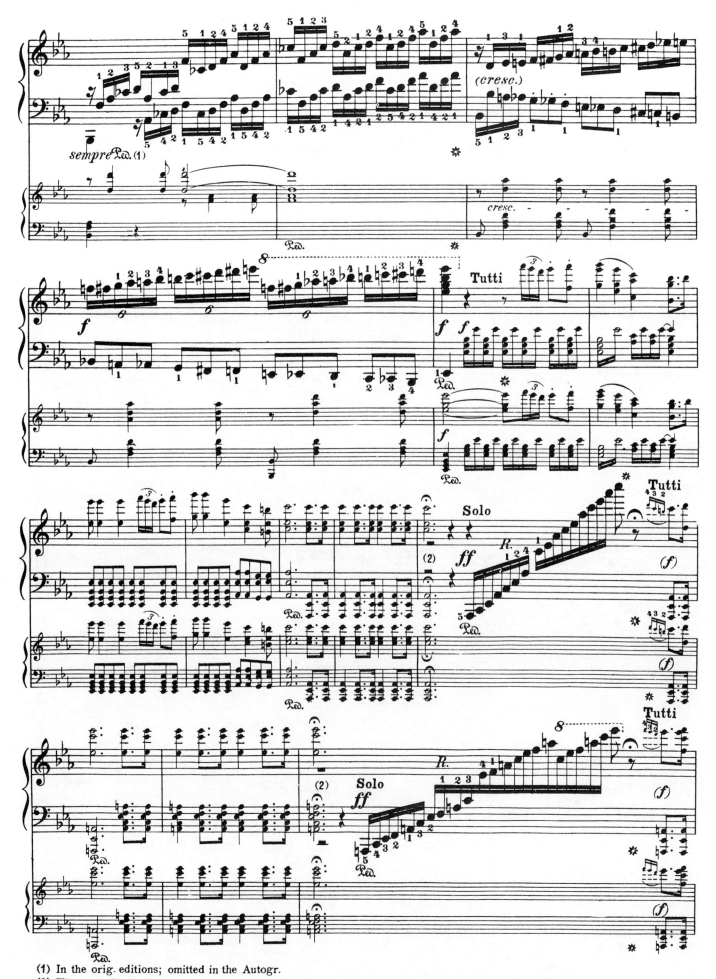

(1) In the orig. editions; omitted in the Autogr.
(2) The rests in the right hand follow the Autogr.; those in the left hand are also in the orig. editions.

(1) Omitted in the Autograph.

(2) Acc. to the orig. editions ✲. In the Autogr. this measure, and the next 15, are lacking; they are given in a copy, but without the piano-part.

(1) All following staccato signs in this passage are omitted in the Autogr. (but given in the orig. editions).

II.

Adagio un poco moto. ($\flat$ = 66; Czerny $\flat$ = 60)

(1) $\mathbb{C}$ (not $\mathbf{C}$) acc. to the Autogr. and the orig. editions.

(1) The dashes of prolongation here and for the following *cresc.* are only in B and C.

(1) Originally 𝄞. (2) Prolongation of the slurs acc. to Autogr.

(1) >> acc. to the Autogr.

semplice poco tenuto (1)

Rondo (acc. to Czerny, ♩.=96)
Allegro.

III.

p

ff

Allegro.
sempre pp

(1)   (2)   (3)   (4)   (5)

p

espressivo

nachdrücklich (3)

(6)   (7)   (8)

(1) This mark, *"semplice poco tenuto,"* together with the appertinent holds, is omitted in the Autogr. In the next measure, editions B and C contain between the lines, below (and belonging to?) the *ff,* the words *"ma non troppo."* In A this addition is lacking; indeed, there was no room for it in the corrected plate after "Allegro." In the Autograph there stood originally, after "Rondo Allegro" the words *"non tanto,"* which were later crossed out (probably by Beethoven himself) with pencil.

(2) *"sf,"* though perhaps wholly justifiable on practical grounds, is given by none of our sources in the Solo, for the principal theme; but is found in the arrangement (p.137), and in the Tutti.

(3) This addition, lacking in the original editions, is found on the extreme lower margin of the Autograph.
  [energetic, forceful]

(1) Fingerings of the orig. editions; but not marked until the repetition of the passage on p. 146.

(2) Facilitated: [musical notation] originally written [notation].

(3) The Autogr. gives: [musical notation] These arpeggio-signs are all omitted in edition A; also in the parallel passage. In edition B the chords are crossed, as in the Autogr., but in different places.

(1—1) In the Autogr. (not in the orig. editions) all the note-heads of this entire arpeggio are (intented to be) of the same size.

(2) Slurs acc. to the parallel passage in the Autogr. *Cf.* also p.147.

(1) Acc. to the Autogr.

(2) "*p*" in the orig. editions; indistinct in the Autogr. *(Ped.?)*.

(3) Edition B has the 5th, ed. A (probably by mistake) the 4th finger.

(4) Added note in recent editions; originally only *c*. Also *cf.* p. 25 of our edition of the C-minor Concerto.

(1) In the Autograph, *"dolce"* (not given in the orig. editions).

(1) Here *f* in the Autogr.' (not given in the orig. editions). The *c* is an added note (as on pp.138 and 142.

(1) This *f* omitted in the Tutti-arrangement of the Autogr. The *g♯* in the bass is an added note, as in the parallel passages.

(1) Fingering only in the Autograph.
(2) "*Staccato*" in the Autogr., and in editions B and C. The two following in B and C only.

(1) In the orig. editions *sf* is repeated here. The Autograph has only a comprehensive sign of repetition ("*sim.*"), which probably refers only to the notes.

(2) This *p*, repeated here in the orig. editions, appears to have been the sole such sign in this place in the Autograph; the preceding *p* was in pencil, then retraced in ink.

(1) Fingering of the orig. editions.

(1) (f - p), given here in analogy with the parallel passage on p.134, is omitted both in the orig. editions and the Autogr., this f not being repeated in the latter even for the orchestral instruments.

(2) The *upper* slur is also in the orig. editions (given in them *under* tr).

(1) Facilitated: etc.

(2) *Stacc.* in the orig. editions (and the parallel passage); not given in the Autograph.

(1) Autogr. gives *p* (omitted in the orig. editions).

(1) The *p* in the Tutti-arrangement of the Autogr. is omitted in the orig. editions; — in all four sources, the *p* is omitted for Cor.; in the Autogr., on the other hand, the bassoon has the direction "*Solo, dolce.*"

(1) This f, not quite as distinct in the Autogr. as the simultaneous f for the orchestral instruments (but in no event belonging to the Tutti-arrangement – Corni), is omitted in the orig. editions.

(2) More recent editions publ. by Br. & H., among them that by Moscheles, give p here and also two measures further on; just here a leaf of the Autograph is missing.

(1) The repetition of this *sf* is omitted in the Autogr., and also in the printed Orig. Quartet Parts (edition C), to which we are able to refer.

END OF EDITION